T0400549

FASCINATING ☑LISTS ABOUT NATURE'S GROSSEST AND GREATEST

Heather E. Schwartz

CAPSTONE PRESS
a capstone imprint

Published by Capstone Press, an imprint of Capstone
1710 Roe Crest Drive, North Mankato, Minnesota 56003
capstonepub.com

Library of Congress Cataloging-in-Publication Data is
available on the Library of Congress website.

ISBN: 9798875228261 (hardcover)
ISBN: 9798875231940 (paperback)
ISBN: 9798875231957 (ebook PDF)

Summary: Plug your nose and brace yourself for some of the
smelliest, slimiest, grossest, and greatest things ever found
on planet Earth. Easy-to-read lists entice reluctant readers
and draw in book lovers who love being totally grossed
out! Digestible lists are separated into chapters to make
information clear, and full-color images paired with eye-
catching designs spark curiosity.

Editorial Credits
Editor: Marissa Bolte; Designer: Kay Fraser;
Media Researcher: Svetlana Zhurkin;
Production Specialist: Katy LaVigne

Image Credits
Capstone: Kay Fraser (design elements), cover and
throughout; Getty Images: ©Juan Carlos Vindas, 31, 500px/
Wilson Khor, cover (flower), 19, Antagain, 10, Beachmite
Photography, 20, Geerati, cover (bat), Kevin Schafer, cover
(bottom right), Michel Viard, 29, ScrappinStacy, 12, Tuan
Tran, 13, Zakharchenko, cover (butterfly); Shutterstock:
Andrey Gudkov, 14, BlueBarronPhoto, 28, CRS Photo,
22, doliux, cover (bottom left), Eric Metz, 30, Evelyn D.
Harrison, 21, finchfocus, 17, fivespots, cover (Gila monster),
IanRedding, 7, Kamil Srubar, 8, Konstantin Aksenov, 18,
Leonardo Viti, 23, olko1975, 24, Oussama enniour, 9,
Peterpancake, cover (snake), petrdd, cover (frog), Piokal, 4,
Robert Harding Video, 26, Saifullahphtographer, 16, Stephen
Lew, 27, Stephen Moehle, 5, Sukpaiboonwat, 11, Thierry
Eidenweil, 15, velis hadi, 25, Wirestock Creators, 6

Printed and bound in the USA. 6307

TABLE OF CONTENTS

CHAPTER 1
UNUSUAL HABITATS AND HIDDEN CREATURES

Nature is fascinating and beautiful. It can be gross and creepy too! Want to learn more? Check out these lists!

PHENOMENAL FORESTS

- Crooked Forest, Poland—where trees grow curved and crooked
- Redwood Forests, California—legendary land of the world's tallest trees
- Hoia-Baciu Forest, Romania—famous for alien sightings and hauntings by ghosts

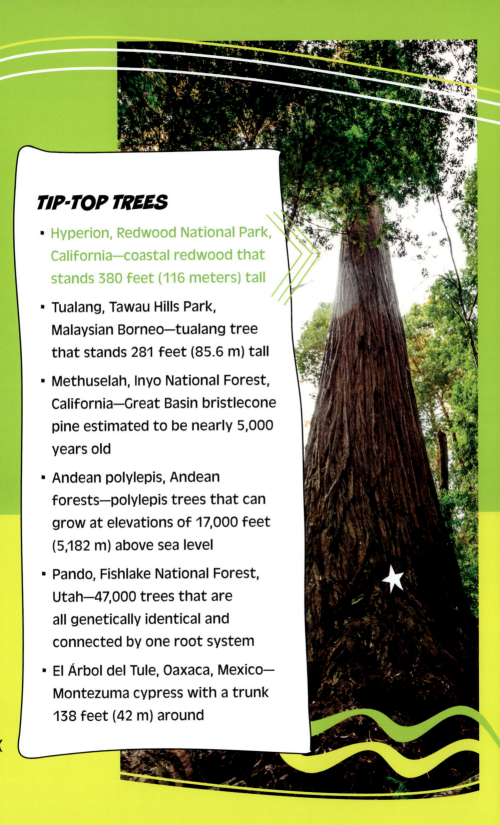

TIP-TOP TREES

- Hyperion, Redwood National Park, California—coastal redwood that stands 380 feet (116 meters) tall

- Tualang, Tawau Hills Park, Malaysian Borneo—tualang tree that stands 281 feet (85.6 m) tall

- Methuselah, Inyo National Forest, California—Great Basin bristlecone pine estimated to be nearly 5,000 years old

- Andean polylepis, Andean forests—polylepis trees that can grow at elevations of 17,000 feet (5,182 m) above sea level

- Pando, Fishlake National Forest, Utah—47,000 trees that are all genetically identical and connected by one root system

- El Árbol del Tule, Oaxaca, Mexico—Montezuma cypress with a trunk 138 feet (42 m) around

LEAFLIKE INSECTS

Trees are cool, and insects know it! Here are some bugs that make themselves look like leaves to hide.

- brimstone butterfly
- giant leaf insect
- dead-leaf grasshopper
- Indian oakleaf butterfly
- leaf katydid

PLANTLIKE BUGS

- buff-tip moth—looks like a birch twig
- walking stick—looks like a green or brown stick
- moss mimic stick insect—looks like moss
- orchid mantis—looks like a pink, white, or purple orchid

HIDING IN PLAIN SIGHT

- South American leaf fish—swims along like a drifting leaf
- Malayan leaf frog—blends into the forest like a brown leaf
- nightjar—a gray, brown, or reddish-brown bird that blends in with the trees
- ringed plover—a tan and black bird that hides among pebbles on the beach

EXTRAORDINARY ENVIRONMENTS

- Pacific Ocean's underwater hot springs—home to tubeworms and giant clams
- Atlantic Ocean's underwater hot springs—home to eyeless shrimp
- Antarctic ice—home to microbes that have been frozen there for millions of years
- outer space—Eight-legged micro-animals called tardigrades or water bears were brought to the International Space Station by NASA astronauts!

BEASTS WHERE THEY DON'T BELONG

- Hawaii has rock-climbing goby fish.

- The Bahamas have pigs that swim at the beach!

- Mexico has snakes that hang from the ceiling of a cave.

- Scotland has become home to some Australian wallabies.

- Brooklyn, New York, has monk parakeets that fly freely.

- San Francisco, California, has a large parrot population.

- Czechia has brown bears living in a moat around a castle.

- Italy has goats living in a dam.

- Morocco has goats living in trees!

CHAPTER 2

UNBELIEVABLE BEHAVIOR

Sometimes, animals don't behave like we think they should. They do their own thing!

ANIMALS THAT ACT LIKE PEOPLE

- Baby elephants suck their trunk, just like some human babies suck their thumb.

- Tigers seek revenge. Watch out!

- Raccoons can pick locks.

- Muriqui monkeys hug each other.

- Male kangaroos flex their arm muscles. Are you impressed?

TOOTS AND POOTS

- Manatees fart to control how much they float or sink.
- Herring communicate through fart sounds.
- Sloths don't fart. When gas builds up, their body reabsorbs it.

BIZARRE BATHROOM BEHAVIOR

- Dogs aim their pee high on trees to trick other dogs into thinking they're bigger.
- Cougars spread seeds with their poop.
- Wombat poop is shaped like cubes.
- Lobsters pee out of their face.
- Crabs pee out of their eyes.
- Sloths poop only once a week.
- Bears don't poop at all while hibernating.

DYNAMIC DEFENSES

- Opossums fake their own death.

- Africanized bees smell like bananas before they attack.

- The kinkajou turns its feet around to run backward.

- Vultures puke to scare off predators.

- Hoatzins, also called stink birds, smell like cow manure.

TOUGH GUYS

You wouldn't want to face down one of these frightening creatures!

- Goliath birdeater tarantulas—the largest spiders in the world
- gharials—also called fish-eating crocodiles, they can reach 16 feet (5 m) long!
- vampire bats—Yum, blood for dinner again!
- giant African millipedes—up to a foot (0.3 m) long, with hundreds of legs

IMPRESSIVE MIGRATIONS

- Monarch butterflies travel 3,000 miles (4,800 kilometers) from Canada to Mexico.

- Humpback whales swim more than 4,970 miles (8,000 km) from cold to warmer waters.

- Salmon swim 250 miles (400 km) against the current through rapids and waterfalls.

- Arctic terns fly about 25,000 miles (40,000 km) each year—maybe much more!

- Wildebeests roam in groups of more than 1.5 million through Tanzania and Kenya.

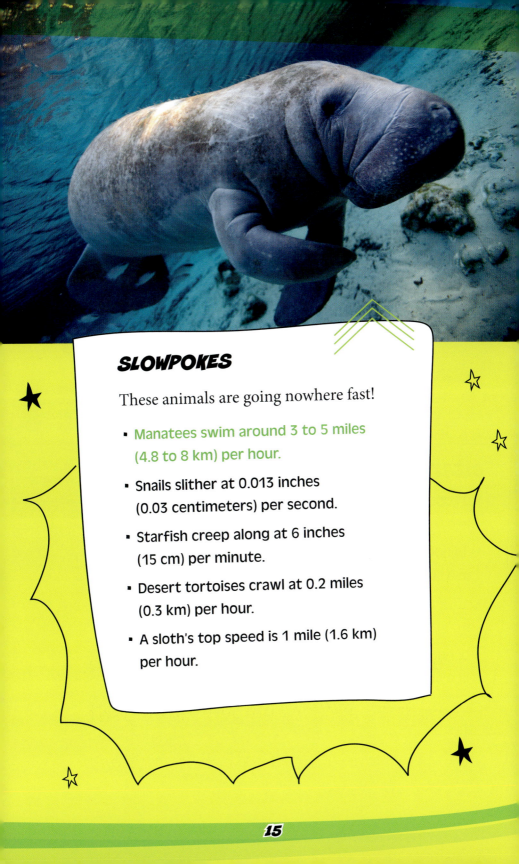

SLOWPOKES

These animals are going nowhere fast!

- Manatees swim around 3 to 5 miles (4.8 to 8 km) per hour.

- Snails slither at 0.013 inches (0.03 centimeters) per second.

- Starfish creep along at 6 inches (15 cm) per minute.

- Desert tortoises crawl at 0.2 miles (0.3 km) per hour.

- A sloth's top speed is 1 mile (1.6 km) per hour.

CHAPTER 3

FASCINATING FEATURES

From heartless creatures to flowers that mimic monkeys, you have to see them to believe them!

BIZARRE BITES

- 27,000: number of teeth in a slug's mouth
- 14,000: number of teeth in a snail's mouth
- 10: length in feet (3 m) of a narwhal's tooth
- 0: number of top teeth in a cow's mouth

WHAT'S INSIDE?

- You can see a glass frog's organs through its skin.
- A blue whale's heart weighs about 400 pounds (181 kilograms). That's the size of a gorilla!
- Octopuses have three hearts.
- Earthworms have no heart.
- A zebrafish can regrow its heart.

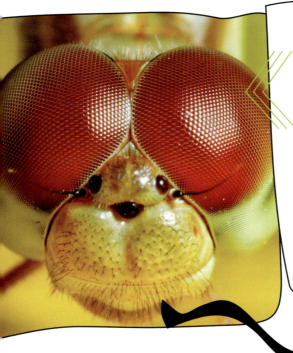

EYE SEE YOU

- most eyes: Dragonflies have five eyes with up to 30,000 lenses!
- biggest eyes: Colossal squid eyes can be 11.8 inches (30 cm) across.
- no eyes: Bacteria don't have eyes, but their whole body acts like an eyeball.

WORLD'S SMALLEST ANIMALS

Weigh in! Which creatures are itty-bittiest?

- pygmy rabbit—1 pound (454 grams)
- pygmy marmoset—4.2 ounces (119 g)
- speckled padloper tortoise—0.4 pounds (181 g)
- bee hummingbird—0.004 pounds (2 g)
- slender blind snake—0.003 pounds (1.4 g)

WORLD'S BIGGEST BEASTS

- heaviest insect: Goliath beetle
- largest bird: ostrich
- longest animal: giant ribbon worm
- tallest animal: giraffe
- heaviest animal: blue whale

TOP 5 LARGEST FLOWERING PLANTS

- monster flower—weighs up to 15 pounds (6.8 kg)

- sunflower—grows up to 30 feet (9.1 m) tall

- talipot palm—has flowering branches 19 to 26 feet (5.8 to 7.9 m) long

- Pando—a colony of more than 47,000 trees with a singular root system weighing 13 million pounds (5.9 million kg)

- Posidonia—a colony of flowering seagrass in the Mediterranean Sea that covers 15,000 square miles (38,849 square km)

BIGGEST FAMILIES

- 32: largest mammal litters (tenrecs, which look kind of like hedgehogs)
- 50: most bird eggs per nest (ostriches)
- 29,100: most insect eggs (Australian ghost moths)
- 100: most reptile eggs per nest (sea turtles)

BIGGEST BABIES

- African elephants—300 pounds (136 kg)
- blue whale calves—6,000 pounds (2,722 kg)
- "Babe," the heaviest newborn human baby—22 pounds (10 kg)

TOP 7 DEADLIEST PLANTS

- rosary pea
- water hemlock
- deadly nightshade
- white snakeroot
- castor bean
- oleander
- tobacco

TOP 5 MOST POISONOUS CREATURES

- box jellyfish
- Gila monster
- stonefish
- platypus
- European mole

UNUSUAL PLANTS

Some people think all plants have roots and leaves. But that's not true! Here are some plants that don't have either.

- liverwort
- Thurber's stemsucker
- Hydnora africana
- moss

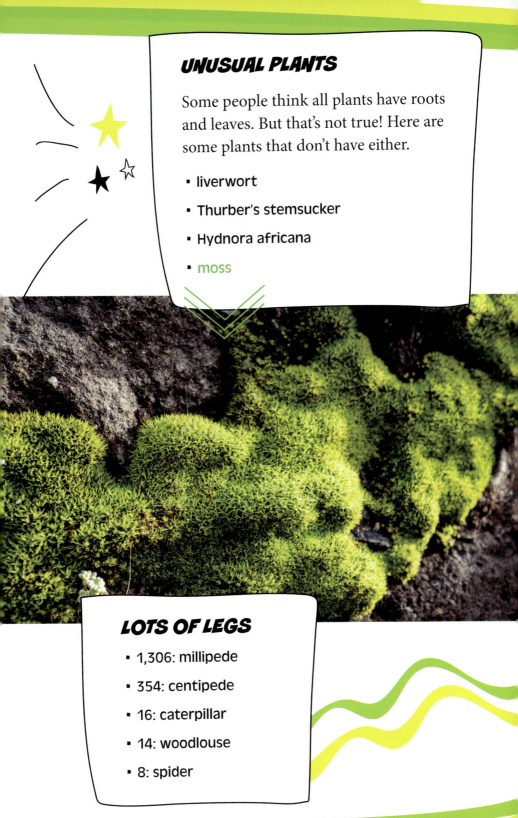

LOTS OF LEGS

- 1,306: millipede
- 354: centipede
- 16: caterpillar
- 14: woodlouse
- 8: spider

IN DISGUISE: DRESSING UP

These animals "dress up" like other animals.

- The spicebush swallowtail caterpillar looks like a small snake or tree frog.
- Hoverflies look (and act) like bees, but they don't sting.
- Owl butterflies have a wing pattern that looks like an owl's face.
- Milk snakes are harmless, but their red, yellow, and black stripes make people think they're venomous coral snakes.

IN DISGUISE: PLANTLIKE ANIMALS

- leaf sheep sea slug
- leafy sea dragon
- leaf-tailed gecko
- sea anemone

IN DISGUISE: ANIMAL-LIKE PLANTS

Can you guess how these plants got their names?

- rabbit succulent
- bee orchid
- dolphin succulent
- moth orchid
- parrot flower
- cobra lily
- monkey face orchid

CHAPTER 4

EXTRAORDINARY ABILITIES

Still want more? Check out the talents
Mother Nature gave these brilliant beasts.

SINGULAR SKILLS

- Pacific barreleyes can rotate their eyes to look through their own transparent head.
- Reindeer eyes change color depending on the season.
- The immortal jellyfish changes form to grow old and then age backward.
- Sea cucumbers turn themselves liquid to hide from predators.
- Marine iguanas can stop their own heart.

WEAPONIZED BODIES

These animals throw things at their enemies!

- Velvet worms can shoot sticky slime up to 2 feet (0.6 m).
- Octopuses grab weapons with their arms. Then they create jets of water to "throw" them.
- Sea cucumbers can shoot water or goo out of their butt.
- Horned lizards shoot blood from their eyes.
- Elephants use their trunks to pick up and throw objects.

ANIMALS THAT REGROW BODY PARTS

- axolotl: limbs
- deer: antlers
- Mexican tetra fish: tissue
- salamander: tail
- sea cucumber: organs
- starfish: arms

WEIRD WAYS TO HIBERNATE

- Snails cover themselves with slime.
- Garter snakes get into groups of hundreds or even thousands.
- Wood frogs freeze solid. They thaw out in the spring!
- Common poorwills hibernate in rock piles.

NAPTIME SNACKS

How do animals survive without snacks during hibernation?

- Fat-tailed dwarf lemurs store fat in their tails.
- Wild hamsters store food and occasionally wake up to eat.
- Bats eat as much as possible before hibernation. They survive on stored fat.

TOP 5 LONGEST NAPS

Some animals take sleep very seriously! Some do it every winter. Others hunker down whenever food is scarce.

- 210 days: free-living wood frog
- 240 days: Arctic ground squirrels
- 310 days: Australian eastern pygmy possum
- 334 days: edible dormouse
- 3 years: land snails

ON-THE-JOB SKILLS

- Crows can learn to count out loud.
- Ants can detect tumors in mice.
- Bees can find explosives.
- Ferrets can carry electrical cables.
- Rats can sniff out land mines.

TOP 5 EASY-TO-TRAIN PETS

- dogs
- rats
- rabbits
- fish
- birds

ANIMALS THAT ACT LIKE OTHER ANIMALS

- tree ocelot—makes sounds like a monkey
- mimic octopus—imitates jellyfish, crabs, sea snakes, and other animals
- male superb lyrebird—mimics other birds' calls
- alligator snapping turtle—wiggles its tongue like a tasty worm to lure prey
- wasp beetle—makes jerky movements to imitate a flying wasp
- Macroxiphus—ant-mimicking cricket nymphs
- atlas moth—moves like a cobra to scare off predators

MORE INFO FANATIC BOOKS!

ABOUT THE AUTHOR

Heather E. Schwartz is an author, singer, and performance artist based in upstate New York. She loves writing because she loves learning new things and brainstorming creative ideas. A few sights she would like to see from this series include Cat Island, mammatus clouds, and Prada Marfa. She'd rather not experience spider rain! She lives with her husband and two kids, and their cats, Stampy and Squid.